DIN DAN DON IT'S CHRISTMAS

PICTURES BY JANINA DOMANSKA

GREENWILLOW BOOKS

A DIVISION OF WILLIAM MORROW & COMPANY, INC. / NEW YORK

1 2 3 4 5   79 78 77 76 75

Library of Congress Cataloging in Publication Data
Main entry under title: Din dan don, it's Christmas.
Text is a rendition of an anonymous Polish Christmas carol.
SUMMARY: A procession of birds and people wend their way to
the Christ Child's creche. [1. Carols, Polish. 2. Christmas music]
I. Domanska, Janina.   PZ8.3D597   783.6'5'09438   75-8509
ISBN 0-688-80003-3   ISBN 0-688-84003-5 lib. bdg.

DIN DAN DON
IT'S CHRISTMAS

The speckled duck plays the bagpipes.

Din dan don she plays.

The gander and the turkey beat the drums.

Din dan don they beat.

The rooster blows the trumpet.

Din dan don he blows.

The nightingale sings his song.

Din dan don he sings.

The goldfinch joins the chorus.

Din dan don he trills.

The sparrows watch over the manger.

They chirp in the rafters.

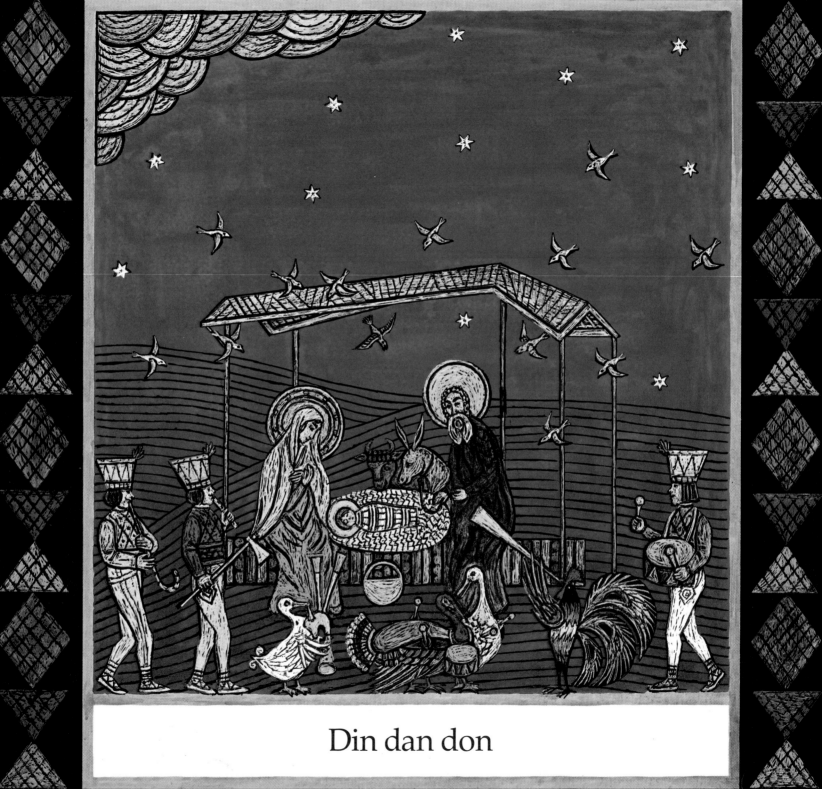

Din dan don

chirp the sparrows.

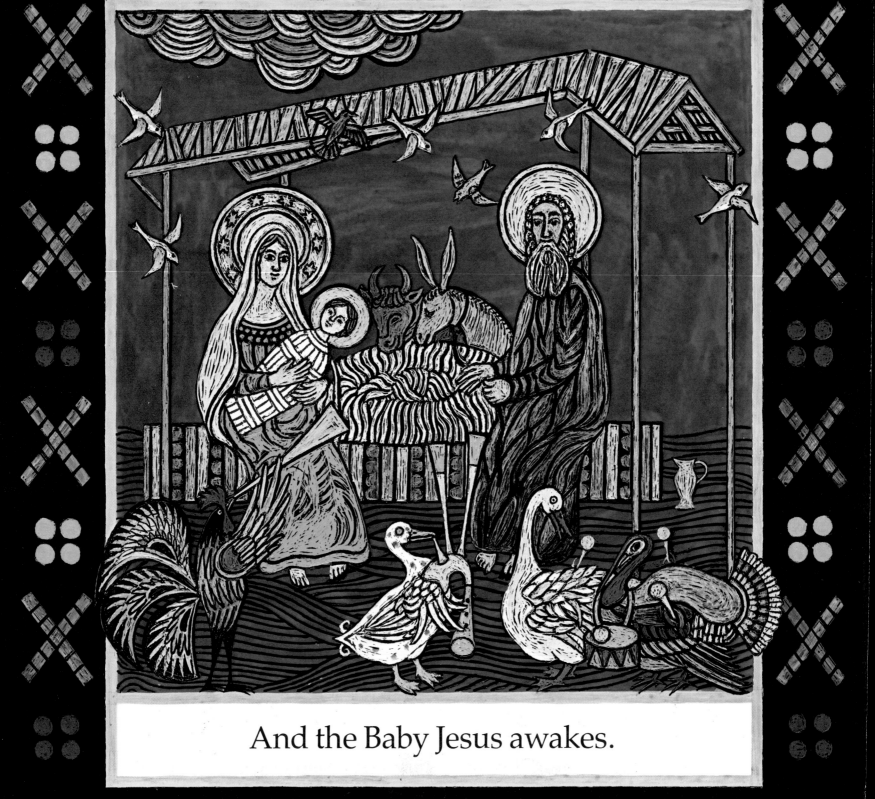

And the Baby Jesus awakes.